IT \

In paradise there are many black angels
But only one that is as graceful and beautiful as you
You hold the key and keys to my heart because your sweet
music fills me with joy
Peace – true peace
True harmony
Truth

You are friend
Time
My one true King

MICHELLE JEAN

In all I do I see the goodness in you
The goodness in songs
Music

You are my choice of truth
True love
True peace and harmony

You are my world of hope that one day the evils in the spiritual realm will be no more.

My hope that one day you will infinitely and indefinitely shut all forms of spiritual wickedness and evil down so that spiritual evil cannot affect us in the physical plain and world anymore.

You are my hope that the strife and wars in the spiritual realm will indefinitely stop for more than infinite and indefinite lifetimes and generations to come.

You are my hope – true hope for a better today and tomorrow including future.

You are my true hope of goodness and truth and that is why I chose you Good God.

Michelle Jean

My days are filled with music now and in all that I do I give you thanks Good God.

I give you thanks because you truly love me
Made me a little bit like you

You are my goodness and truth
That's why I more than infinitely truly love you

You are my good scented rose
The beautiful crystals that I more than love and adore
Beautiful crystals that I more than love to see

You are my crystal clear waters that is void of pollution and chemicals

Void of human and animal waste

You are my good heaven and paradise
My perfect and good universe
Perfect and good life

So to you my true love, I do chose you because our love is beyond the goodness of life.

It is more than real
It is me and you.

Michelle Jean

My darling and friend – Good God
I don't want to change me for you
I want to be just as good as you in all that I do

I know the distance between me and you – us but on this
day we are extremely close. On this day I dedicate Heaven
Chose You by R. Kelly to you.

You are more than my Valentine. You are my friend
My infinite chosen one

We are close
Beyond close
We are forever ever because I am truly truthful to you no
matter how much I bicker and nitpick with you.

Because you chose me and you've chosen me to be by your
side and assist you. I truly thank you for all you've done for
me including truly thank you for the good people you've
given me. I more than love you because you are my truth
hence you are the truth in me.

You are dear hence without you I would be lost.

Once again thank you for being you and being so patient
with me.

Michelle Jean

In all I do, I need you my friend and Good God
In all I do, I need your protection over physical and spiritual evil
– wickedness and death.

I need your goodness of truth above all Good God; hence no one
can live without you.

No one can live without your goodness.

I must choose good life and that good life is you hence I choose
you.

I choose time and the goodness of time because time is good life
and time is you hence good life and the goodness of life.

Dear God – Good God you've shown me many things but in all
you've shown me in the physical we've forgotten about spiritual
wickedness that constantly wage war on man – humanity.

Good God without you we are lost hence we need to work
together in unison to shut down spiritual evil and wickedness
including death. We can no longer allow spiritual evil to wage
war on humanity – humans. Yes it's good to shut down physical
evil and this will be done but we cannot shut down physical evil
alone. We must shut down spiritual evil also.

Spiritual evil is deadly and sinful hence we must shut spiritual
evil down. The spiritual world does affect us as humans; hence
evil comes down from this realm. Good God, we need you hence I
am asking you for help to shut down spiritual evil also.

I know you have the power and ability to shut the wickedness in the spiritual realm down and this morning, I am sincerely and truly asking you to shut all forms of spiritual evil and wickedness down.

Good God evil hath no place in our world nor does it have a place with man but somehow the portal has been open and we have to close it down now.

Good God, I cannot fight alone hence he the one that is always with me. You must shut spiritual evil down because it is affecting me and you. I cannot complain to man and ask man to shut this realm down because man do not know how to. Only you, hence I am truly coming to you with my true love and truth.

I am depending on you to aide me in my request of truth.

Good God, truth does not hurt, evil hurts and I truly don't want evil to hurt me anymore. I need you Good God, I truly need you.

On this day October 08, 2013 I sincerely ask you and petition you in true love to shut down all forms of spiritual wickedness and evil so that it does not hurt me and your good and true people anymore.

Michelle Jean

In my darkest hour I see you standing there with outstretched hands.

You pulled me close and told me you are there for me
You truly love me and I'm your true love.

In your eyes I see the truth
I see the pain of not having me there with you all the time
I see your desire and truth of me

I know I am your world
So between the miles in a universe pure and serene true, I will meet you.

Be with you

You are my key to forever
You are my forever ever and I give you my word that I will never leave you. I will always be true and truthful to you even on my sinful and doubtful days.

You are my stay
My true world
My trillions, billions including millions, hundreds and thousands

You are my true name sake hence we are a true and good family.

Michelle Jean

In all that I see, I see a world that is ending
I see war and strife, hence TV
I see children suffering
I see adults suffering
I see nations suffering and all governments do is lie and tell
more lies to keep their people satisfied. Hence time will tell
for the wicked and evil man including women and child.

In all that I see, I see a system that is based on untruth –
lies and corruption
A system designed to kill
A system that do kill
Control and dominate

A system that has turned humanity against God – Good
God

A system that breads lies and sells lies
A system designed by the Babylonians
Hence the Babylonian system of things – lies and death

All this I see and more but yet helpless to help
Helpless to spread the truth
Helpless to heal
Spread true love

In all I do, I do in truth but where is the truth in the
spiritual world?

Where is the truth in humanity?

Where is the truth all around?

The spiritual world is riddled in sin just like the physical world and no one in the spiritual world is willing to do anything about it.

Each world must be clean and true for humanity to have true peace, hence the fighting in the spiritual world continues, cannot cease to exist period.

The sins of man have and has affected both worlds but in this affecting, how does humanity cope?

How do we stop the spiritual plagues that affect us here on earth?

How do we stop the spiritual plagues that affect our lives on a daily basis?

How do we stop the destruction of self, this world and humanity by the spiritual wicked – evil?

How do we truly move on when the spiritual world is so messed up – plagued by demons that do all to destroy in the living as well as in death – heaven – the spiritual world?

Many questions have I Good God because both the physical and the spiritual must be clean. You cannot have cleanliness in one and not have it in the other.

We need to know what to do Good God because spiritual thwarting and pressure do affect the human psyche – body.

It does affect your health on a massive scale. I know this first hand because the power of evil in the spiritual realm is that strong – unlimited. I say unlimited because evil does not cease once the flesh is dead. Evil moves on towards the spiritual realm and wreaks havoc there as well.

God – Good God how can we sustain and maintain ourselves is self cannot maintain self in the physical. I mean the spiritual affect us so what is the purpose of just cleaning self without cleaning the spirit and moving away from all that is wicked and evil.

The spiritual world does distort and like I've said, I need absolute truth from you. So how do we bypass the evils of the spiritual world and connect in truth, true peace and harmony?

I do not want us to stop at the spiritual because I know you do not reside in the spiritual. You are in another universe void of space and time. You are in truth, the truth of time which is a time in time at a specific point in time and I need to connect to that specific point and time in time. I need to be fully clean to reach you but how can I fully reach you when the spiritual world hinders me from connecting to you.

You are my true right but how can you be when I am being hindered by evil spirits?

Tell me Good God, how fair is this to me? You know the truth of me and all that is within me, but you continue to let evil hinder me from reaching you.

Truly help me to shut down spiritual evil because like I said, spiritual evil affect the psyche as well as our physical body. Spiritual evil and or energy decays – burns and is ugly. This decaying energy is strong and powerful and because of this, spiritual evil drains you. Drains your energy so that you become ugly like them. Yes spiritual evil causes you to sin and become ugly. This I know Good God but we need you. We need your help. We need your truth and beauty.

We need your true peace and harmony to defeat spiritual wickedness.

We can no longer be governed by spiritual evil Good God because not all loves dirty – unclean – filthy and unclean spirits and homes.

Good God, I chose you hence my way should be clean and clear of all spiritual evil and wickedness at all times.

God – Good God, why let me continue to be a victim of spiritual wickedness?

I know the sword of death because I've seen it but yet I am not allowed to use it. I cannot dirty my hands in the spiritual realm. Just as we are not to take a life in the physical, we are not to take a life in the spiritual. I know this but Good God what good am I if spiritual wickedness reach me all the time?

What good are you to me if you continue to make spiritual evil and wickedness reach me?

What are you telling me?
Are you telling me, no matter what we do to make ourselves clean we cannot get away from evil?

If so then Good God, then none of us can or will be clean. Nor will we attain you or reside with you.

I don't know but we truly need to discuss spiritual wickedness and evil Good God because spiritual wickedness and evil is more deadlier than physical wickedness.

Spiritual wickedness bound good. Traps good and keep good locked up.

Spiritual holds are not easily broken and when you are bound, you are bound and cannot be loosed. You are bound for a time because spiritual evil hath time to do its dirty will. If you are not strong you will fail, lose not just your sanity but your life. You know the truth and have the truth but evil uses the by any means necessary to keep you from spreading the truth and saving others. You know this Good God hence I say you to do want your messengers to succeed against evil. Hence your poor track record throughout history.

I know the fight I face in the spiritual realm hence I am coming to you to shut down the spiritual evils that surrounds me as well as hinders me and others. There are still good people on this earth Good God and we need to save them before it's too late.

You cannot say heaven chose me and have the evils of heaven – the spiritual universe kill me – destroy and control me.

You cannot say you love us so and have spiritual evil kill us at will.

You cannot say you love us so and have spiritual evil dominate and control us.

You cannot say you love us so and have spiritual evil lead us to hell with their lies.

You cannot say you love us so and have spiritual evil destroy our physical body by bombarding our physical body with negative energy all the time and at will.

Tell me something Good God. What about our true and good life with you?

If death uses the physical and spiritual to destroy, what are you doing?

What are you truly doing to save us?
What are you truly doing to help us?
How are you protecting us?

Good God no one should have to face hell on earth then to face it again in the spiritual plain.

I know good is separated from evil hence it's the evil ones in the spiritual realm that wreak havoc in the physical world.

I know if evil cannot get into your abode no one is going to get in. He will destroy it all. But with all that said Good God, why are you not with us?

Why are you not helping me to defeat physical and spiritual evil?

Yes it's good to say you are there but how are you there for me when evil wreaks havoc on my body. My body is tired and in need of true rest – a vacation from it all.

I don't know Good God because nothing makes sense.

I cannot comprehend why you would allow evil to dominate and control in this way?

I cannot comprehend why you allow evil to enslave us.

Yes I know it's the choice we made but look at it. You created the universe in goodness and in truth and to have someone destroy it like that does not make any sense to me.

You cannot continue to let people that do not care about you destroy all that you created?

You cannot continue to let people that do not care about you destroy your good life and reputation.

You cannot continue to let people that don't care about you dominate and control your people.

I know it took one but what about you and the truth of you?

What about your true happiness as well as the truth of you?

Earth is dominated and controlled by lies in both worlds but yet you continue to let this happen. Yes 24 000 years had sin and death but why?

Why give them that one day when you know one day to man is not one day in the spiritual world – realm?

You knew the pain and suffering humanity would face. You knew the chaos that would be on earth.

You knew we could not govern self. We would just contribute to the chaos. You knew all of this but yet you let evil continue on its merry way.

You aided sin, evil and death and now look at the damage. You had no right to give evil sin and death a home. You were wrong because not all life is sentient nor is all life true. You know this but yet you continue to hold out for something. What that something is you are the only one that knows because I truly don't know on this day.

I truly don't know why you keep holding on to people that means you no good.

I know I cannot see your future and I have to live with what is being shown to me but I still say you are wrong when it comes to humanity.

Some people willingly sin.
Some people don't give a crap. All they think about is ego and self. Look at the world today Good God and tell me what did it profit you to create negative energy?

Death is not pretty so why leave negative energy in the equation? ***And truly don't give me the opposites attract bullshit because that don't wash with me. I truly love goodness, good true and clean people. These are the people I want and need to attract. Good clean and honest people that work to uplift each other as well as help each other in a positive way.***

Clean attract clean hence when clean live with dirty they are never happy and their spirits are cross. You see this in the way I complain about my children's messiness. I don't want to live with them because of nastiness. When your children are nasty and people come into your home and see this nastiness, they think you are nasty. You know this Good God hence I want and need to leave my nasty children. I so cannot live with them because they upset my spirit daily with their nastiness.

In a dirty and evil society – system you cannot get this meaning you cannot get cleanliness. You knew the consequences of your actions Good God hence you must admit fault and guilt for your wrongs.

Yes I know you cannot be wrong, but on this day see with me and just bare with me even if you cannot give me right.

Pain and suffering is something neither of us like so why did you allow evil to reach your people? I know your true people are living with you and we are the children of sin. Children that want to come home but did we have to learn the hard way?

Good God this way on earth is not nice.
Spiritual beating is not nice.

Good God, the pain on earth does not compare to spiritual pain and you know this. So tell me what are we going to do when we reach the spiritual world?

<u>The judgement there is harsher than the judgement of earth. Hence I tell you, I do not want to go to the spiritual world because I know for an infinite fact that you do not reside in the spiritual world.</u> *You are in another universe and time – time zone. This time zone I cannot get to because my wavelength cannot connect to yours. I do not know how to connect the time and you are not showing me how to connect to you.*

Good God, I need to know how to connect to you one on one because you are my strength. I so do not need or want the hindrance from the spiritual realm anymore.

Good God can't we find a different way to communicate.

So lead me to all the good songs you need me to dedicate unto you so that we can be happy in truth and in true love.

Yes I know you truly love music. So do I, but the good ones I need to dedicate to you. And yes I infinitely know that Satan was not a musician. His last name was Singh, Sing and Singer. Now music is distorted and corrupted with lying thieves that steal our true and good birthright and made it the devils own. But it's only a matter of time when we will regain our true heritage and sing good music unto you once again. The devil's music must go down to the pits of hell with evil making the world a better place to live in.

The good songs I need to serenade you with. Yes this will be our mode of communication because it seem lately you want and need good music.

I can't write music nor can I sing so let my poetry be your songs of truth and true joy – true love.

Let my words speak to you of truth and true love
True joy and happiness not just for a second but for all eternity because I know eternity cannot end. I need you to be truly happy so that you can make me truly happy because somehow I think you've lost all your happiness.

So on this day find truth, true love and hope including true love in all that I write for you.

I know one day we will meet on the mountain of good life and yes when I get there I am still going to pinch you. This I must do so truly let me pinch you and say truly thank you for truly loving me as well as securing and protecting me.

Good God, these little things I need in truth because you are my love and true love.

So now you know that it would be you and yes I do choose you in all that I do be truly happy as well as lift your head up high in joy.

Enjoy the rest of the day and truly do good unto me by shutting down all spiritual evil. I truly need to get to you and I cannot do that if spiritual evil surrounds me as well as hinder me from getting to you.

Michelle Jean

Ah my family today is different because I don't know where to start. I've been dreaming about music lately. I know the music of today is filled with evil and how to correct this, I truly do not know. Although you have good artists – musicians out there the majority of them are not clean hence the music industry need to be cleaned up.

These artists that say they represent Good God are all fake. None represent you Good God because they make sacrifices unto death – the Abrahamic Order of sin.

The Rasta Artists are no different because after Bob Marley and Peter Tosh goof reggae music is no more. These Rasta artists live to deceive and kill with their music. Hence I've told you, all that Bob and Peter did to spread the truth, the now artists in the reggae industry have and has undone what they did.

Many sing about the happenings in the country but yet none truly give back to their community. The community they grew up in. Many palava pan wey dem have while they see hunger in the streets and do nothing about it. Politicians and grown ass men rape young children and none have condemned these happenings. Politicians give the ghetto youths guns and ammunition to kill each other and none do anything about it. Many more they see and do and do nothing about it. But it's a matter of time that all will be taken from them. They will lose it all because they aide sin to kill their homeland and people and truly woe be unto them because this is their first woe. Thus saith the lord meaning it is so.

All it takes is one but that one refuses to stand up. Buying prostitutes and whores serve their personal purpose and not the good and true help of the people of their land.

Everyone wants it all but when it comes to true giving no one want to help.

WE TALK ABOUT THE CORRUPTED SYSTEM OF THE WORLD BUT REFUSE TO ACKNOWLEDGE THAT WE ARE APART OF THIS CORRUPTED SYSTEM. HENCE THESE SYSTEMS ARE FUELED BY US – EACH INDIVIDUAL.

WE REFUSE TO ACKNOWLEDGE THE FACT THAT WE ARE THE ONES TO CREATE THESE CORRUPTED SYSTEMS.

WE ARE THE ONES WHO VOTED THESE WICKED AND EVIL PEOPLE INTO OFFICE SO WE TOO HAVE TO TAKE THE BLAME FOR THE CORRUPTED SYSTEMS OF THE WORLD.

WE TALK ABOUT CIVILITY BUT WE THE INDIVIDUAL CREATED UNCIVILIZED SYTEMS. HENCE WE CANNOT BLAME OTHERS WITHOUT BLAMING SELF.

We the individual or citizens of the world are corrupted hence the saying thief no like fi si thief carry long bag. We see the shit that is happening in the world and instead of changing self and do better, we run with the system of corruption and complain later.

A corrupt system cannot change if the individual does not want to change. You must change before change can come about.

As individuals we want change to come but refuse to change self. Change cannot come without changing you. You have to change you before change can come. Come on now.

We talk about change but change how?
Change for the better or for the greater evil?

The choice is yours hence you have to make the right choice.

If you want a better system then elect good people and hold them accountable for the wrongs they do in office. If that person is not working for the betterment or better good of you and your country then vote him or her out of office. Do not re-elect him or her into office. **WE ALL KNOW THAT EVIL DESTROYS – KILLS and instead of moving away from wicked and evil systems we continue to wallow in it and complain.** You elected these people so you the person or individual are to blame as well.

Hence you the individual is held accountable for the politician or person you elected into office. Sin does not go one way it is all around hence the judgement. You voted slackness into office as well as put up with slackness.

Like I've told you, if you sin not evil will die. Evil can cease to exist but as long as we sin, evil will never stop – die. We are the ones that need to clean up self including spirit if we want to grow up and see Good God.

Sin – evil feed off you hence I've told you, the greatest weapon sin has and have against Good God is humans. We sin then turn around and complain to Good God about our hurt and pain. Well if you don't want pain stop sinning then. Come on now.

We've become so sinful that billions are slated to die shortly. And none of us can blame Good God for this because it was not Good God that sinned, you did.

You knowingly sin and when things have and has gone wrong we expect Good God to fix our problems for us.

Trust me I complain about the nastiness of my children but God – Good God can't fix their nastiness because it was not God – Good God that made them nasty. If I had lain with someone that was clean they would be clean and this is my reality. Yes I teach my children about cleanliness and yell at them but if a child is bent on keeping their nasty ways there is absolutely nothing you can do to change them and make them clean. Yes I pray but what do you do when prayer does not work? I have to learn to walk away from them and this is what I am looking forward to right now. I have to do what Good God did to Eve (Evening). Yes it's easier said than done but I have to. This is the reality of things. As parents we can only do so much hence I cannot live in nastiness. A nasty home is damned nasty and I need to reside with Good God in a clean true and good home. I chose him hence my surroundings must be clean and this is what he's trying to tell me. Hence on this day October 09, 2013 I more than overstand.

All that we do must be clean hence I've let go of my negative feelings. You'll know and see them in words. Like I said, I cannot be a hypocrite because my world is not governed by me alone, it is governed by my ancestral bloodline and it is that strong and deadly at times

I cannot love I have to truly love hence the differentiation between the two.

You may not like me.

You can hate me for the words in all these books but I truly do not care. At the end of the day as long as Good God truly loves me then I am okay.

Like I said, we want lies and we do live in lies and expect Good God to accept us for the lies we live in

and tell and he Good God cannot do that. No liar is found in his abode because his abode is not based on lies but on truth.

No one wants to hear the truth hence we embrace lies and this is wrong. I've told you Good God would infinitely never ever send someone to die for your sins because your sins are yours and they are recorded in your record book.

But but.

There are no buts. I've told you the good seeds that Good God has and have given me I am responsible for them. I have to take care of them hence the goodness I do must go towards saving them as well. I cannot just save me because Good God did not give me, me alone. He gave me them. Seeds hence these seeds must grow up in goodness not just for me and them but for Good God also.

Many of us want lies hence Bob Marley sang Time Will Tell to teach you but you could not comprehend. Well shortly you will comprehend and when you think you're in heaven you're living in hell. This will be the reality of billions shortly. So if you are a billionaire that think you can buy heaven think again because to you I dedicate TIME WILL TELL BY BOB MARLEY. YOU THINK YOU'RE IN HEAVEN BUT YOU'RE LIVING IN HELL LITERALLY. Many of you have and has signed your name on the dotted line and trust me you're hell bound because like I've said, Good God does not reside in the spiritual death and sin does. The demons of hell does. So truly woe be unto you on earth as well as in the spiritual realm shortly.

Hell will be your home shortly and you will burn. Like I've said, if the lie did not work for Eve (Evening) how the hell do you expect it to work for you?

Your billions cannot save you in the grave because no tree belongs to death – Satan. Hence your money cannot save you because it is made from trees – paper amongst other resources that was stolen from Mother Earth. Resources none of you replenished, so truly woe be unto you because for all that you take from earth without just cause, you will pay for and pay dearly.

Like I've said, what I do is not just for me. Good God must enjoy my goodness and truth and if he does not enjoy it then something is wrong.

I cannot live to destroy because I do not love destruction. I will however destroy evil because evil hurts. Evil causes pain and no one should feel pain. No one should live in sin just to die to go to hell and die again.

Yes I have bones to pick with other countries and I've voiced them to Good God and you because you're all my witness of truth, hence these books that you are reading. I cannot change what is ordained. No that's a lie, I can, but do I want to? No. I will not change any of these words to suit man or God – Good God. I stand by them until the end of evil time. Evil hath an end people and I've told you this. Even when evil dies, I will not change these words because I am infinitely truthful to Good God.

AND AGAIN I WILL TELL YOU. GOOD GOD DOES NOT LOCK ANYONE OUT OF HIS ABODE. SO LONG AS YOU ARE LIVING YOUR LIFE IN GOODNESS AND TRUTH, YOU CANNOT BE LOCKED OUT OF HIS ABODE BECAUSE GOOD GOD TRULY, MORE THAN TRULY LOVES TRUTH.

Truth is your key to him not death hence truth is everlasting life.

If you do not have truth then you will not have everlasting life.

Yes it's October 09, 2013 and the spirit is tired in many ways hence I truly need a vacation by 2014. If not by the end of 2013 because I cannot take what the spiritual forces have done to my body.

My body needs rest and I have to get it even if it's for a week or two.

My body needs proper rest and it is crying out for it.

It needs some sexual healing too but that's for a different book when I go buck wild.

Man I so don't want to go to the states but if I could I would. No not really because there's nothing I would like to do there apart from buying panties and bras. Maybe shoes. Pity I didn't have a sugar daddy to buy me some real sexy sexy ones hence I have to design my own and market them to you. Trust me when I do this, perversion will have nothing on me because I will take my mind to the limit sexually. And no; no skinny people need to apply because I refuse to design for them. Only big and bold, yes sexy, sexy woman and cougars like me. Well not a cougar but if I was trust me .... no let's forget it because this is so not the book for it.

Yes I am tired and in need of some true pampering.
In need of true love
In need of a true vacation somewhere where I don't do have to do anything. Just sleep and drink and have fun. No alcohol need to apply because we are so not friends. Body truly rejects you – alcohol.

Ah yes the day has just begun and things are so different family.

I have not told you about my spiritual dreams. I've not shared them with you because they are not easily shared and I truly don't know if you can comprehend them. Hence I've truly omitted them from these books.

Most of these dreams consist of me fighting and running – escaping my enemies that are trying to kill me in the spiritual realm. Yes this is why my body is so tired in the physical because spiritual fights are taxing on the body in the physical.

They are hard to explain as I've said because these fights do not occur in earth or on earth. They're usually on another planet. Hence I've told you man knows not the technology on the moon. Nor do they know the technology in the spiritual realm. This realm is highly advanced. What we conjure up or write about in the movies are child's play in the spiritual realm. You dear to dream but in the spiritual world or realm these dreams are a reality. Man's advancement is nothing compared to the advancement in the spiritual realm.

Man I do not know where to begin because this dream is different, it's a spiritual dream.

The first half, I cannot take you into it because I am not allowed to. Just know that it had to do with me fighting. And no I've never used weapons in these fights. It's usually my enemies that use weapons. They are the ones trying to take my life but somehow I am never caught – they cannot catch me to kill me. These dreams are not on earth like I've told you. They are usually on a distant planet hence I know the fighting that I have to face in this world. Meaning I know what spiritual evil is trying to do to me. My death has and have been commissioned by death long ago hence

I've told you what death does not complete in the living, they must complete in death. But death cannot take me because Good God is my stay hence I know my purpose in this world. I have to carry it out despite the backlash by the evil ones including my own and the different races of earth.

All I can do is run to Good God when the backlash comes. So the first half of the dream I am not allowed to tell you like I've said. Just know that it had to do with me fighting – running for my life. I cannot explain the first half then. Know that getting water from a pipe with a bag that had a hole in it to feed this dog – brown dog was in the dream. Some of the water came out of the bag but not all. This dog looks like no dog on earth. It was a good dog hence I was feeding it water. Yes there was other people – white in the dream that thought I wasn't going to make it – give the brown dog water because the bag had a hole in it. But despite the hole the dog got water. Was fed. That's all I can tell you. After that somehow I was in this place. I don't even know if it was earth because I did not recognize the land – country. All I knew was I escaped the spiritual fight and was in another place where these ladies and I were playing tennis. One lady had to be extra and hit the ball over the fence. We were using regular green tennis balls. We had a good amount. Suffice it to say I looked up and when I looked up I saw this planet. It had light coming out of it and it had cracks. Let me see if I can find a picture on Google for you to see what I am talking about. Go to Google Images and find 3840 x1200 – tumlol.com. This image is what the cracks and light look like. There wasn't one crack.

There was more but you get the idea. The colour of the planet is the exact same colour of the image. Size a tad smaller. This planet was a billion light years from us. I am going to say earth because we had green grass and we were playing tennis on green grass. And no for those who are wondering if it was daytime. It was not daytime but night time. Do not say strange because our spiritual eyes are different from our physical eyes. Everything in the spiritual predominantly is night time. Night sky of light and dark hence I've told you there is light in the darkness hence we cannot comprehend or understand nor overstand certain things.

Onwards I go.

I say this planet or moon if you want and now you know what it looks like. Suffice it to say these ladies could not see this planet or moon if you chose moon.

Like I said, this planet is 1 billion light years from us. Keep in mind that I escaped from the fighting and now I am someplace else. I was safe but not safe enough. Seeing the planet all I saw was this one spaceship coming down to earth. It landed on earth where we were playing tennis. When the ship landed it was like a pod – like unto a pea pod but made of cloth. Cream cloth is the best way to describe it. If you can remember those olden days telephones of cream. That colour was the colour of the pod. 300 x 225 Weekly World News.com is a good picture but 3840 x 2400 Wall Save.com is the perfect picture. The top is more round like the top in 300 x 225 Weekly World News.com. There are no pictures in pea pod that I can use to describe the image of the ship when it landed.

Upon the space ship landing people began to disappear. I did not see the people disappearing but they did. Meaning these beings took their body and used it. All that was left was their clothes. Keep in mind that I escaped from another planet and I guess it was me they were seeking because one of them – a black lady got close to me as if she wanted to possess me. There were three of them. All black. Two males and one female and the colour of choice is black as always when it comes to true spiritual evil – death.

I've told you the colour of death – demons when they come to earth is black. They cannot use any other colour apart from black when they come to possess you – kill you. Because I've told you there are no possessions just like that.

I've told you, you have to give yourself over to death – these demons before they can possess you. And I've told you how this is done.

This possession in this particular dream is my death. My death has and have been commissioned in the spiritual realm and I told you this above hence I will always have a fight. I know my fight hence I talk to Good God in a certain way sometimes. You cannot do what I do because you are not ordained to do so nor do you have a true relationship with Good God.

Suffice it to say the black girl dressed in black took the life of someone. She had to gain access to their clothing. She came near to me to do her will but I caught her and she turned into a key. You know those L shaped key. Go to Google and type in L shaped Key. The sixth key is the exact key. 360 x 360 Global Sources.com is the image. Like I said, she turned into this key. The turned she turned into this key I don't know where the power came from but I bent the key in half. Seeing what I did the two men that was with her turned into the same key and came towards me. They were in the grass slithering towards me and I picked them up and bent them as well. I literally had three (3) keys in my hand that I bent. **_The bending I bend I threw all 3 bent keys into the fire._** Don't ask me where the fire came from. All I know is that I threw all 3 keys into the fire. I do not know if they died because in the dream I was not sure. So if you know what this dream means please let me know. I know death walks in threes hence the degree of death is three meaning the highest degree death can go to is three. There cannot be a fourth or fifth. There can only be three. Hence the 4th and 5th including sixth degrees of evil – sin and death is incorrect. Hence above is corrected. There can only be a maximum of three degrees because there are only 3 deaths. You cannot put Eve or Satan in this degree because they are not true sin – true death. So no, the 3xy rule does not apply hence I am correcting myself on this day. So truly take the 3xy out of the equation of sin because *it does not apply. 1x2y (2yx) applies but not 3xy. 3Y applies but not 3xy. How you see death changes hence you have to know death and true death as well as destructive death. I will not explain them if you do not know them because they are confusing to explain if you do not know the spiritual realm. And I've confused you with the dream already.*

And no you cannot use the four and twenty elders because the twenty four elders represent the time frame of sin. Each prince or elder had one thousand years to deceive man – humanity hence you have army time or army clock representing them.

So to those who have more than three degrees in your lodge man organizations you are not representing sin or death you are just representing you – your leader.

And no you cannot say you are Satanists because true evil is female in the spiritual realm and the physical realm.

These are the gods of evil – sin.

FOR GOOD TRUE GOOD GOD IS FEMALE IN THE PHYSICAL REALM AND MALE IN THE SPIRITUAL REALM. HENCE I'VE TOLD YOU GOD – GOOD GOD IS FEMALE IN THE PHYSICAL AND MALE IN THE SPIRITUAL REALM.

Evil cannot change but good changes. Good grow and go up to Good God whereas evil goes down to death – die.

The dream continues hence this next part I am going to go to Good God because he's the only one that I can bug. I am going to get mad Good God because I constantly tell you that I do not want to see this man and you keep letting me see him. I know you are telling me that evil is in music but how do I clean this evil up?

I know you have evil singers in the music industry and you don't like it. Many of these musicians are into voodoo and the lodge man thing which hurts you but what can I do? You too have to remember that we all have choices and many have chosen evil over you.

I know the evil that you are showing me in Jouvert – Soca Music of Grenada but I have to admit the music is intoxicating and it does invoke the spirit. Hence Duppy Art or Voodoo Music in my book. I know I have to be careful in certain things but Good God .... never mind I have to leave Jouvert Music alone because it infinitely has nothing to do with you.

But Good God this man is fine.......yes I will walk away before I lose you. I know my boundaries so I will leave things alone. The horns of the dead and the masks of the dead are not nice because they are our sins hence many of us have and has lost our souls without knowing it.

Good God, I know you have to teach me about evil but does it have to be him. I know the evil in him hence the lies he told but then you have your reasoning hence I cannot truly blast you.

Yes evil sings so truly continue to guide me to the right music that you need your people to listen to – hear. I know I can't always give music but Good God why not? Oh well I will leave this alone hence I will stay away from Grenadine Jouvert Music and this man no matter how tempting he is.

Wow. Yes the waistline and winery.
Wow. But I have to let go.

So now I have to go because I've gone far enough with this book.

Off track as usual but there is nothing I can do about it.

There is more to come hence these little mini books.

Sight is coming back people hence I see the travels in my house.

Oh well don't think I want to stand and talk to ghosts face to face. No for real. Some you cannot see their faces because they don't let you see them. Some are dressed in white and you just glimpse the colour passing through. Why me I do not know but like I've told you what some death looks like.

Sometimes you don't want to close your eyes because some are that grotesque to look upon. Some are like animals and trust me these animals are freakishly gross. More grotesque than the human ones at times.

So truly take care of yourself. You need your life so protect it and as the dreams come I will give them to you. Not as much spiritual ones but my dreams as given to me.

Spiritual dreams pertaining to the moon or this planet is hard.

Michelle Jean

Please check out my 50+ other books on lulu.com.

For example:

The New Book of Life – Judgement
Blackman Redemption – The Death of Russia
Blackman Redemption – The Rise and Fall of Jamaica
Lose to Win and many more.

Truly thank you for supporting me and if you can, buy the artwork of these artists. Yes I have to buy them because I have one that is dear to me and I have to get this picture and hang it on my wall.

Michelle Jean